CHRISTMAS

POPE BENEDICT XVI

SPIRITUAL THOUGHTS SERIES

Edited by Lucio Coco

United States Conference of Catholic Bishops
Washington, DC

OTHER TITLES IN THE SPIRITUAL THOUGHTS SERIES

Pope Benedict XVI: Spiritual Thoughts
in the First Year of His Papacy
The Eucharist
Family
Following Christ
Mary
The Priesthood
The Saints
St. Paul
Sickness
The Word of God
Young People

First printing, November 2011
ISBN 978-1-60137-194-2

CONTENTS

o welcome the Savior and to recognize him in the humble Child lying in a manger. This is the mystery of Christmas.

Benedict XVI

PREFACE

The Mystery of Christmas[1]

he desire we all carry in our hearts is that in the midst of the frenzied activity of our day the forthcoming Feast of Christmas may give us serene and profound joy to make us tangibly feel the goodness of Our Lord and imbue us with new courage.

At Christmas God truly became the "Emmanuel," the God-with-us from whom no barrier nor any distance can separate us. Thus, in that Child, God became close to each one of us, so close that we are able to speak intimately to him and engage in a trusting relationship of deep affection with him, just as we do with any newborn baby.

In that Child, in fact, God-Love is manifest: God comes without weapons, without force, because he does not want to conquer, so to speak, from the outside, but rather wants to be freely received by the human being. God makes himself a defenseless Child to overcome pride, violence and the human desire to possess. In Jesus God took on this poor, disarming condition to win us with love and lead us to our true identity. We must not forget that the most important title of Jesus Christ is, precisely, that of "Son," Son of God; the divine dignity is indicated with a term that extends the reference to the humble condition of the manger in Bethlehem, although it corresponds uniquely to his divinity, which is the divinity of the "Son."

---

1   This preface is taken from the General Audience of December 23, 2009.

His condition as a Child also points out to us how we may encounter God and enjoy his presence. It is in the light of Christmas that we may understand Jesus' words: "Unless you turn and become like children, you will never enter the Kingdom of Heaven" (Mt 18:3). Those who have not understood the mystery of Christmas, have not understood the crucial element of Christian life. Those who do not welcome Jesus with a child's heart, cannot enter into the Kingdom of Heaven. Let us pray the Father to grant us that simplicity of heart which recognizes the Lord in the Child.

Benedictus XVI

CHRISTMAS

1. *Hope*

Christ, the Son of God brings to the dark, cold and unredeemed world into which he is born a new hope and a new splendor. If man lets himself be moved and enlightened by the splendor of the living truth that is Christ, he will feel inner peace in his heart and will become a peacemaker in a society that so longs for reconciliation and redemption.

Address to pilgrims from Lower Austria
December 12, 2008

I. THE GIFT OF ADVENT

2. *Visit*

The essential meaning of the word *adventus* was: God is here, he has not withdrawn from the world, he has not deserted us. Even if we cannot see and touch him as we can tangible realities, he is here and comes to visit us in many ways.

Homily at First Vespers of Advent
November 28, 2009

3. *Presence*

Advent, this powerful liturgical season that we are beginning, invites us to pause in silence to understand a presence. It is an invitation to understand that the individual events of the day are hints that God is giving us, signs of the attention he has for each one of us.

Homily at First Vespers of Advent
November 28, 2009

4. *Waiting*

The question is: Is the humanity of our time still waiting for a Savior? One has the feeling that many consider God as foreign to their own interests. Apparently, they do not need him. They live as though he did not exist and, worse still, as though he were an "obstacle" to remove in order to fulfill themselves. Even among believers—we are sure of it—some let themselves be attracted by enticing dreams and distracted by misleading doctrines that suggest deceptive shortcuts to happiness. Yet, despite its contradictions, worries and tragedies, and perhaps precisely because of them, humanity today seeks a path of renewal, of salvation, it seeks a Savior and awaits, sometimes unconsciously, the coming of the Savior who renews the world and our life, the coming of Christ, the one true Redeemer of man and of the whole of man.

General Audience
December 20, 2006

5. *Preparation* (1)

Christmas is a privileged opportunity to meditate on the meaning and value of our existence. The approach of this Solemnity helps us on the one hand to reflect on the drama of history in which people, injured by sin, are perennially in search of happiness and of a fulfilling sense of life and death; and on the other, it urges us to meditate on the merciful kindness of God who came to man to communicate to him directly the Truth that saves, and to enable him to partake in his friendship and his life. Therefore let us prepare ourselves for Christmas with humility and simplicity, making ourselves ready to receive as a gift the light, joy and peace that shine from this mystery.

General Audience
December 17, 2008

6. *Preparation* (2)

Thus, to prepare oneself for Christmas means to be committed to building the "dwelling of God with men." No one is excluded; everyone can and must contribute in order to make this house of communion more spacious and beautiful.

Angelus
December 10, 2006

7. *The Immaculate*

In today's consumer society, this period [of Advent] has unfortunately suffered a sort of commercial "pollution" that risks changing its authentic spirit, marked by recollection, moderation and joy, which is not external but intimate. It is thus providential that almost as a portal to Christmas there should be the feast of the one who is the Mother of Jesus and who, better than anyone else, can lead us to know, love and adore the Son of God made man. Let us therefore allow her to accompany us; may her sentiments prompt us to prepare ourselves with heartfelt sincerity and openness of spirit to recognize in the Child of Bethlehem the Son of God who came into the world for our redemption. Let us walk together with her in prayer and accept the repeated invitation that the Advent liturgy addresses to us to remain in expectation—watchful and joyful expectation—for the Lord will not delay: he comes to set his people free from sin.

Angelus
December 11, 2005

II. THE RESPONSE OF MARY

8. *Two comings*

"In the first [coming]," St. Bernard wrote, "Christ was our redemption; in the last coming he will reveal himself to us as our life: in this lies our repose and consolation" (*Discourse 5 on Advent*, 1). The archetype for that coming of Christ, which we might call a "spiritual incarnation," is always Mary. Just as the Virgin Mother pondered in her heart on the Word made flesh, so every individual soul and the entire Church are called during their earthly pilgrimage to wait for Christ who comes and to welcome him with faith and love ever new.

Homily at Vespers of the First Sunday of Advent
December 2, 2006

9. *Making room*

Thus, it is Mary who tells us what Advent is: going forth to meet the Lord who comes to meet us; waiting for him, listening to him, looking at him. Mary tells us why church buildings exist: they exist so that room may be made within us for the Word of God; so that within us and through us the Word may also be made flesh today.

Homily for the Second Sunday of Advent
December 10, 2006

10. *Hail, Mary*

The first word on which I would like to meditate with you is the Angel's greeting to Mary. In the Italian translation the Angel says: "Hail, Mary." But the Greek word below, "*Kaire*," means in itself "be glad" or "rejoice." . . . This is the first word that resounds in the New Testament as such, because the Angel's announcement to Zechariah of the birth of John the Baptist is the word that still rings out on the threshold between the two Testaments. It is only with this dialogue which the Angel Gabriel has with Mary that the New Testament really begins. We can therefore say that the first word of the New Testament is an invitation to joy: "Rejoice, be glad!" The New Testament is truly "Gospel," the "Good News" that brings us joy.

Homily for the Fourth Sunday of Advent
December 18, 2005

11. *Full of grace*

"Full of grace" . . . is Mary's most beautiful name, the name God himself gave to her to indicate that she has always been and will always be the *beloved*, the elect, the one chosen to

welcome the most precious gift, Jesus: "the incarnate love of God" (*Deus Caritas Est*, no. 12).

Angelus
December 8, 2006

12. *The Lord is with you*

God, who became present here on earth, truly dwells in Mary. Mary becomes his tent. What all the cultures desire—that God dwell among us—is brought about here. St. Augustine says: "Before conceiving the Lord in her body she had already conceived him in her soul." She had made room for the Lord in her soul and thus really became the true Temple where God made himself incarnate, where he became present on this earth.

Homily at Mass for the Solemnity of the Assumption
of the Blessed Virgin Mary
August 15, 2006

13. *New creation*

The narrative of the Annunciation illustrates God's extraordinary courtesy (cf. Mother Julian of Norwich, *Revelations* 77-79). He does not impose himself, he does not simply pre-determine the part that Mary will play in his plan for our salvation: he first seeks her consent. In the original Creation there was clearly no question of God seeking the consent of his creatures, but in this new Creation he does so. Mary stands in the place of all humanity. She speaks for us all when she responds to the angel's invitation. . . .

Mary said, "Let it be done to me according to your word." And the Word of God became flesh. When we reflect on this joyful mystery, it gives us hope, the sure hope that God will continue to reach into our history, to act with creative power so as to achieve goals which by human reckoning seem impossible.

Homily at Vespers in the Basilica of the
Annunciation in Nazareth
May 14, 2009

14. *The Visitation*

Mary went to see her elderly cousin Elizabeth, whom everyone said was sterile but who instead had reached the sixth month of a pregnancy given to her by God (cf. Lk 1:36), carrying in her womb the recently conceived Jesus. She was a young girl but she was not afraid, for God was with her, within her. . . . Jesus' presence filled her with the Holy Spirit. When she entered Elizabeth's house, her greeting was overflowing with grace: John leapt in his mother's womb, as if he were aware of the coming of the One whom he would one day proclaim to Israel. The children exulted, the mothers exulted. This meeting, imbued with the joy of the Holy Spirit, is expressed in the Canticle of the *Magnificat*.

Address during the prayer meeting for the conclusion
of the Marian month of May
May 31, 2005

15. *By faith*

Mary "sees" the work of God in history with the eyes of faith. This is why she is blessed, because she believed. By faith, in fact, she accepted the Word of the Lord and conceived the Incarnate Word. Her faith has shown her that the thrones of the powerful of this world are all temporary, while God's throne is the only rock that does not change or fall. Her *Magnificat,* at the distance of centuries and millennia, remains the truest and most profound interpretation of history, while the interpretations of so many of this world's wise have been belied by events in the course of the centuries.

> *Address at the Marian vigil for the conclusion*
> *of the month of May*
> *May 31, 2008*

16. *The* Magnificat

Why exactly did God choose from among all women Mary of Nazareth? The answer is hidden in the unfathomable mystery of the divine will. There is one reason, however, which is highlighted in the Gospel: her humility. . . . In the *Magnificat,* her canticle of praise, the Virgin herself says: "My soul magnifies the Lord . . . because he looked upon his servant in her lowliness" (Lk 1:46, 48). Yes, God was attracted by the humility of Mary, who found favor in his eyes (cf. Lk 1:30). She thus became the Mother of God, the image and model of the Church, chosen among the peoples to receive the Lord's blessing and communicate it to the entire human family.

Angelus
December 8, 2006

_____

_____

_____

_____

_____

_____

_____

_____

_____

_____

_____

_____

_____

_____

_____

III. BE VIGILANT

17. *In expectation*

The spiritual attitude of watchful and prayerful expectation remains the fundamental characteristic of the Christian in this Advent Season. It is this attitude that distinguishes the protagonists of that time: Zechariah and Elizabeth, the shepherds, the Magi, the humble, simple people, above all Mary and Joseph's expectation! The latter, more than any of the others, felt in the first person the anxiety and trepidation for the Child who would be born. It is not difficult to imagine how they spent the last days, waiting to hold the newborn Infant in their arms. May their attitude be our own, dear brothers and sisters!

General Audience
December 20, 2006

18. *Readiness*

Who are those whom God loves, and why does he love them? Does God have favorites? Does he love only certain people, while abandoning the others to themselves? The Gospel answers these questions by pointing to some particular people whom God loves.... Mary, Joseph, Elizabeth, Zechariah, Simeon and Anna ... the shepherds and the Wise Men from the East, the "Magi." ... They were people who were watchful . . . they were ready to receive God's Word through the Angel's proclamation. Their life was not closed in on itself; their hearts were open. In some way, deep down, they were waiting for something; they were waiting for God. Their watchfulness was a kind of readiness—a readiness to listen and to set out. They were waiting for a light which would show them the way. That is what is important for God.

Homily at Mass for the Solemnity
of the Nativity of the Lord
December 24, 2005

19. *The shepherds*

The first thing we are told about the shepherds is that they were on the watch—they could hear the message precisely because they were awake. We must be awake, so that we can hear the message. We must become truly vigilant people. . . . Awake, the Gospel tells us. Step outside, so as to enter the great communal truth, the communion of the one God. To awake, then, means to develop a receptivity for God: for the silent promptings with which he chooses to guide us; for the many indications of his presence. . . . Lord, open the eyes of our hearts, so that we may become vigilant and clear-sighted, in this way bringing you close to others as well!

Homily at Mass for the Solemnity
of the Nativity of the Lord
December 24, 2009

20. *Symbols*

These [symbols of Christmas] include the symbol of light, which is one of the symbols richest in spiritual significance and on which I would like briefly to reflect. In our hemisphere, the Feast of Christmas coincides with the days of the winter solstice, after which the daylight time gradually lengthens, in accordance with the sequence of the seasons. This helps us understand better the theme of light that overcomes the darkness. It is an evocative symbol of a reality that touches the innermost depths of the human being: I am referring to the light of good that triumphs over evil, the light of love that overcomes hatred, the light of life that defeats death. Christmas makes us think of this inner light, the divine light that returns to propose anew to us the proclamation of the definitive victory of God's love over sin and death.

General Audience
December 21, 2005

21. *The tree and the manger*

The tree and the crib are elements of that typical Christmas atmosphere which is part of the spiritual heritage of our communities. It is a climate steeped in religiosity and family warmth which we must also preserve in contemporary society, where the consumeristic rush and the search for material goods alone sometimes seem to prevail.

Address to a delegation from the municipality of
San Martin De Tor in Val Baldia (Bolzano, Italy)
December 14, 2007

22. *The manger*

Every Christmas crib is a simple yet eloquent invitation to open our hearts and minds to the mystery of life. It is an encounter with the immortal Life which became mortal in the mystic scene of the Nativity.

Urbi et Orbi *message for Christmas*
December 25, 2008

23. *Joy*

Joy is the true gift of Christmas, not expensive presents that demand time and money. We can transmit this joy simply: with a smile, with a kind gesture, with some small help, with forgiveness. Let us give this joy and the joy given will be returned to us.

Homily at Mass on the Fourth Sunday of Advent
December 18, 2005

24. *Light*

Let us remember in particular, as we look at the streets and squares of the cities decorated with dazzling lights, that these lights refer us to another light, invisible to the eyes but not to the heart. While we admire them, while we light the candles in churches or the illuminations of the crib and the Christmas tree in our homes, may our souls be open to the true spiritual light brought to all people of good will.

General Audience
December 21, 2005

25. *Gifts*

Christmas is the day when God gave a great gift to us, not something material, but his gift was the gift of himself. He gave us his Son, so Christmas became the feast of gifts.

Greeting to the children of Our Lady Star
of Evangelization Parish of Rome
December 10, 2006

26. *Dwelling place*

In being born among us, may the Child Jesus not find us distracted or merely busy, beautifying our houses with decorative lights. Rather, let us deck our soul and make our families a worthy dwelling place where he feels welcomed with faith and love.

General Audience
December 20, 2006

27. *Wake up!*

"Wake up, O man! For your sake God became man" (St. Augustine, *Sermo,* 185). Wake up, O men and women of the third millennium! At Christmas, the Almighty becomes a child and asks for our help and protection. His way of showing that he is God challenges our way of being human. By knocking at our door, he challenges us and our freedom; he calls us to examine how we understand and live our lives.

Urbi et Orbi *message for Christmas*
December 25, 2005

IV. THE BIRTH OF THE LORD

1. Mystery of Smallness

28. *Close to us*

"To you is born this day in the city of David a Savior, who is Christ the Lord" (Lk 2:11). The Lord is here. From this moment, God is truly "God with us." No longer is he the distant God who can in some way be perceived from afar, in creation and in our own consciousness. He has entered the world. He is close to us.

> *Homily at Mass for the Solemnity*
> *of the Nativity of the Lord*
> *December 24, 2009*

29. *The child*

God is not remote from us, unknown, enigmatic or perhaps dangerous. God is close to us, so close that he makes himself a child and we can informally address this God.

> *Homily at Mass for the Fourth Sunday of Advent*
> *December 18, 2005*

30. *Care*

God is like that: he does not impose himself, he never uses force to enter, but asks, as a child does, to be welcomed. In a certain sense, God too presents himself in need of attention: he waits for us to open our hearts to him, to take care of him.

Address on the Feast of the Holy Family of Nazareth
December 30, 2005

31. *In the grotto*

In the Grotto of Bethlehem God shows himself to us as a humble "infant" to defeat our arrogance. Perhaps we would have submitted more easily to power and wisdom, but he does not want us to submit; rather, he appeals to our hearts and to our free decision to accept his love. He made himself tiny to set us free from that human claim to grandeur that results from pride. He became flesh freely in order to set us truly free, free to love him.

General Audience
December 17, 2008

32. *Holy night*

And the heart of God, during the Holy Night, stooped down to the stable: the humility of God is Heaven. And if we approach this humility, then we touch Heaven. Then the Earth too is made new.

Homily at Mass for the Solemnity
of the Nativity of the Lord
December 25, 2007

33. *Sign*

God's sign is his humility. God's sign is that he makes himself small; he becomes a child; he lets us touch him and he asks for our love. How we would prefer a different sign, an imposing, irresistible sign of God's power and greatness! But his sign summons us to faith and love, and thus it gives us hope: this is what God is like. He has power, he is Goodness itself. He invites us to become like him. Yes indeed, we become like God if we allow ourselves to be shaped by this sign; if we ourselves learn humility and hence true greatness; if we renounce violence and use only the weapons of truth and love.

> *Homily at Mass for the Solemnity*
> *of the Nativity of the Lord*
> *December 24, 2009*

34. *Christmas*

The glory of the true God becomes visible when the eyes of our hearts are opened before the stable of Bethlehem.

> *Homily at Mass for the Solemnity*
> *of the Nativity of the Lord*
> *December 25, 2008*

35. Brothers and sisters

In the Child of Bethlehem, the smallness of God-made-man shows us the greatness of man and the beauty of our dignity as children of God and brothers and sisters of Jesus.

Address to the members of Catholic Action
December 19, 2005

36. Mystery of smallness

God has made himself small for us. God comes not with external force, but he comes in the powerlessness of his love, which is where his true strength lies. He places himself in our hands. He asks for our love. He invites us to become small ourselves, to come down from our high thrones and to learn to be childlike before God. He speaks to us informally. He asks us to trust him and thus to learn how to live in truth and love.

Homily at the Square in front of the Basilica of Mariazell
September 8, 2007

37. Care

Christmas helps us understand that God never abandons us and always comes to meet our needs. He protects us and is concerned with each one of us, because every person, especially the lowliest and most defenseless, is precious in the eyes of the Father, rich in tenderness and mercy.

Address during the visit to the "Gift of Mary" House
conducted by the Missionaries of Charity in the Vatican
January 4, 2008

2. The Wonder of the Incarnation

38. *Our Savior*

Today "our Savior is born to the world," for he knows that even today we need him. Despite humanity's many advances, man has always been the same: *a freedom poised between good and evil, between life and death*. It is there, in the very depths of his being, in what the Bible calls his "heart," that man *always* needs to be "saved." And, in this post-modern age, perhaps he needs a Savior all the more, since the society in which he lives has become more complex and the threats to his personal and moral integrity have become more insidious.

> Urbi et Orbi *message for Christmas*
> *December 25, 2006*

39. *Time of Christ*

With the Incarnation of the Son of God, eternity entered time and human history was opened to absolute fulfillment in God. Time was, so to speak, "touched" by Christ, the Son of God and of Mary, and received from him new and surprising significance: it became a time of salvation and grace.

> *Homily at St. Peter's Basilica on the*
> *Solemnity of Mary, Mother of God*
> *December 31, 2009*

40. *Revolution*

The earthly history of Jesus that culminated in the Paschal Mystery is the beginning of a new world, because he truly inaugurated a new humanity, ever and only with Christ's grace, capable of bringing about a peaceful "revolution." This revolution was not an ideological but spiritual revolution, not utopian but real, and for this reason in need of infinite patience, sometimes of very long periods, avoiding any short cuts and taking the hardest path: the path of the development of responsibility in consciences.

> *Homily on the Solemnity of Mary, Mother of God,*
> *and the 42nd World Day of Peace*
> *January 1, 2009*

41. *Incarnation*

[Jesus] came into the world to bring man back to God, not on the ideal level—like a philosopher or a master of wisdom—but really. . . . For this very reason the Father was pleased with him and "highly exalted" him (Phil 2:9), restoring to him the fullness of his glory, but now with our humanity. God in man—man in God: this is even now a reality, not a theoretical truth.

> *Regina Caeli*
> *May 4, 2008*

42. *Paradox*

In the Child of Bethlehem, God revealed himself in the humility of the "human form," in the "form of a slave," indeed, of one who died on a cross (cf. Phil 2:6-8). This is the Christian paradox. Indeed, this very concealment constitutes the most eloquent "manifestation" of God. The humility, poverty, even the ignominy of the Passion enable us to know what God is truly like.

Homily on the Solemnity of the Epiphany
January 6, 2006

43. *Wonder*

The wonder of the Incarnation continues to challenge us to open up our understanding to the limitless possibilities of God's transforming power, of his love for us, his desire to be united with us. Here the eternally begotten Son of God became man, and so made it possible for us, his brothers and sisters, to share in his divine sonship. That downward movement of self-emptying love made possible the upward movement of exaltation in which we too are raised to share in the life of God himself (cf. Phil 2:6-11).

Homily at Mass in the Upper Basilica
of the Annunciation in Nazareth
May 14, 2009

44. *Kingdom*

Christ brought a Kingdom which is not of this world, yet a Kingdom which is capable of changing this world, for it has the power to change hearts, to enlighten minds and to strengthen wills. By taking on our flesh, with all its weaknesses, and transfiguring it by the power of his Spirit, Jesus has called us to be witnesses of his victory over sin and death.

Homily at Mass in Manger's Square in Bethlehem
May 13, 2009

3. The Truth of Christmas

45. *Feast of light*

The grace of God has appeared. That is why Christmas is a feast of light. Not like the full daylight which illumines everything, but a glimmer beginning in the night and spreading out from a precise point in the universe: from the stable of Bethlehem, where the divine Child was born.

Urbi et Orbi message for Christmas
December 25, 2008

46. *Changing*

Only if people change will the world change; and in order to change, people need the light that comes from God, the light which so unexpectedly [on the night of Christmas] entered into our night.

Homily at Mass for the Solemnity
of the Nativity of the Lord
December 25, 2008

47. *Task*

It is the task of us Christians, with the witness of our life, to spread the truth of Christmas which Christ brings to every man and woman of good will. Born in the poverty of the manger, Jesus comes to offer to all that joy and that peace which alone can fulfill the expectations of the human soul.

General Audience
December 20, 2006

48. *Possibility*

Having become a man, Christ gave us the possibility of becoming, in turn, like him.

General Audience
August 22, 2007

49. *The song of the angels*

The God we contemplate in the crib is God-Love. At this point the message of the angels resounds for us as an invitation: glory "be" to God in the highest of heavens, peace "be" on earth to those whom he loves. The only way to glorify God and to build peace in the world consists in the humble and trusting welcoming of the gift of Christmas: love. The song of the angels can then become a prayer to repeat often, not only in this Christmas season. It is a hymn of praise to God in the highest of heavens and a fervent invocation of peace on earth, which translates into a concrete commitment to build it with our life. This is the duty that Christmas entrusts to us.

General Audience
December 27, 2006

50. *At once*

It tells us that after listening to the Angel's message, the shepherds said one to another: "'Let us go over to Bethlehem' . . . they went at once" (Lk 2:15f.). "They made haste" is literally what the Greek text says. What had been announced to them was so important that they had to go immediately. . . . No doubt they were partly driven by curiosity, but first and foremost it was their excitement at the wonderful news that had been conveyed to them, of all people, to the little ones, to the seemingly unimportant. They made haste—they went at once. In our daily life, it is not like that. For most people, the things of God are not given priority, they do not impose themselves on us directly. And so the great majority of us tend to postpone them.

Homily at Mass for the Solemnity
of the Nativity of the Lord
December 24, 2009

51. *Likeness*

And it is today, in the present, that our future destiny is being played out. It is our actual conduct in this life that decides our eternal fate. At the end of our days on earth, at the moment of death, we will be evaluated on the basis of our likeness—or lack of it—to the Child who is about to be born in the poor grotto of Bethlehem, because he is the criterion of the measure that God has given to humanity.

Angelus
December 9, 2007

52. Great light

This is Christmas—the historical event and the mystery of love, which for more than two thousand years has spoken to men and women of every era and every place. It is the holy day on which the "great light" of Christ shines forth, bearing peace! Certainly, if we are to recognize it, if we are to receive it, faith is needed and humility is needed. The humility of Mary, who believed in the word of the Lord and, bending low over the manger, was the first to adore the fruit of her womb.

Urbi et Orbi *message for Christmas*
December 25, 2007

53. *The swaddling clothes*

"The time came for Mary to be delivered. And she gave birth to her first-born son and wrapped him in swaddling clothes, and laid him in a manger, because there was no room for them in the inn" (Lk 2:6f.). These words touch our hearts every time we hear them. This was the moment that the angel had foretold at Nazareth: "You will bear a son, and you shall call his name Jesus. He will be great, and will be called the Son of the Most High" (Lk 1:31). This was the moment that Israel had been awaiting for centuries, through many dark hours—the moment that all mankind was somehow awaiting, in terms as yet ill-defined: when God would take care of us, when he would step outside his concealment, when the world would be saved and God would renew all things. We can imagine the kind of interior preparation, the kind of love with which Mary approached that hour. The brief phrase: "She wrapped him in swaddling clothes" allows us to glimpse something of the holy joy and the silent zeal of that preparation. The swaddling clothes were ready, so that the child could be given a fitting welcome. Yet there is no room at the inn. In some way, mankind is awaiting God, waiting for him to draw near. But when the moment comes, there is no room for him. Man is so preoccupied with himself, he has such urgent need of all the space and all the time for his own things, that nothing remains for others—for his neighbor, for the poor, for God. And the richer men become, the more they fill up all the space by themselves. And the less room there is for others.

> *Homily at Mass for the Solemnity*
> *of the Nativity of the Lord*
> *December 25, 2007*

54. *Today*

In the silence of that night in Bethlehem, Jesus was born and lovingly welcomed. And now, on this Christmas Day, when the joyful news of his saving birth continues to resound, who is ready to open the doors of his heart to the holy child? Men and women of this modern age, Christ comes also to us bringing his light, he comes also to us granting peace!

> Urbi et Orbi *message for Christmas*
> *December 25, 2007*

55. *Bringing forth Christ*

The Lord can find a dwelling place in our own souls and lives. Not only must we carry him in our hearts, but we must bring him to the world, so that we too can bring forth Christ for our epoch.

General Audience
February 15, 2006

V. THE HOLY FAMILY

56. *Icon*

The first witnesses of Christ's birth, the shepherds, found themselves not only before the Infant Jesus but also a small family: mother, father and newborn son. God had chosen to reveal himself by being born into a human family and the human family thus became an icon of God! God is the Trinity, he is a communion of love; so is the family despite all the differences that exist between the Mystery of God and his human creature, an expression that reflects the unfathomable Mystery of God as Love.

Angelus
December 27, 2009

57. *Duty*

Jesus willed to be born and to grow up in a human family; he had the Virgin Mary as his mother and Joseph who acted as his father; they raised and educated him with immense love. Jesus' family truly deserves the title "Holy," for it was fully engaged in the desire to do the will of God, incarnate in the adorable presence of Jesus.

Angelus
December 28, 2008

58. *Virtue*

From Joseph's strong and fatherly example Jesus learned the virtues of a manly piety, fidelity to one's word, integrity and hard work. In the carpenter of Nazareth he saw how authority placed at the service of love is infinitely more fruitful than the power which seeks to dominate. How much our world needs the example, guidance and quiet strength of men like Joseph!

Homily at Mass at Mt. Precipice in Nazareth
May 14, 2009

59. *Joseph*

St. Joseph's silence does not express an inner emptiness but, on the contrary, the fullness of the faith he bears in his heart and which guides his every thought and action. It is a silence thanks to which Joseph, in unison with Mary, watches over the Word of God, known through the Sacred Scriptures, continuously comparing it with the events of the life of Jesus; a silence woven of constant prayer, a prayer of blessing of the Lord, of the adoration of his holy will and of unreserved entrustment to his providence. It is no exaggeration to think that it was precisely from his "father" Joseph that Jesus learned—at the human level—that steadfast interiority which is a presupposition of authentic justice. . . . Let us allow ourselves to be "filled" with St. Joseph's silence! In a world that is often too noisy, that encourages neither recollection nor listening to God's voice, we are in such deep need of it.

Angelus
December 18, 2005

60. *Prototype*

Mary and Joseph taught Jesus primarily by their example: in his parents he came to know the full beauty of faith, of love for God and for his Law, as well as the demands of justice, which is totally fulfilled in love (cf. Rom 13:10). From them he learned that it is necessary first of all to do God's will, and that the spiritual bond is worth more than the bond of kinship. The Holy Family of Nazareth is truly the "prototype" of every Christian family which, united in the Sacrament of Marriage and nourished by the Word and the Eucharist, is called to carry out the wonderful vocation and mission of being the living cell not only of society but also of the Church, a sign and instrument of unity for the entire human race.

Angelus
December 31, 2006

61. *The Christian family*

Celebrating [today] the Feast of the Holy Family . . . let us fix our gaze on Jesus, Mary and Joseph and adore the mystery of a God who chose to be born of a woman, the Blessed Virgin, and to enter this world in the way common to all humankind. By so doing he sanctified the reality of the family, filling it with divine grace and fully revealing its vocation and mission. . . . The Christian family thus shares in the Church's prophetic vocation: with its way of living it "proclaims aloud both the present power of the Kingdom of God and the hope of the blessed life" (*Lumen Gentium*, no. 35). . . . The good of the person and of society is closely connected to the "healthy state" of the family (cf. *Gaudium et Spes*, no. 47). The Church, therefore, is committed to defending and to fostering "the dignity and supremely sacred value of the married state" (no. 47).

Angelus
December 30, 2007

VI. MARY, MOTHER OF GOD

62. *Mystery*

"Mary kept all these things, pondering them in her heart" (Lk 2:19). The Greek verb used, *sumbállousa*, literally means "piecing together" and makes us think of a great mystery to be discovered little by little. Although the Child lying in a manger looks like all children in the world, at the same time he is totally different: he is the Son of God, he is God, true God and true man. This mystery—the Incarnation of the Word and the divine Motherhood of Mary—is great and certainly far from easy to understand with the human mind alone.

> *Homily at Mass for the Solemnity of Mary, Mother of*
> *God, and the 41st World Day of Peace*
> *January 1, 2008*

63. *Mother of the Redeemer*

Thus, the description "Mother of God," so deeply bound up with the Christmas festivities, is therefore the fundamental name with which the Community of Believers has always honored the Blessed Virgin. It clearly explains Mary's mission in salvation history. All other titles attributed to Our

Lady are based on her vocation to be the Mother of the Redeemer, the human creature chosen by God to bring about the plan of salvation, centered on the great mystery of the Incarnation of the Divine Word.

General Audience
January 2, 2008

64. *The* Theotókos

In the passage from the Letter to the Galatians . . . St. Paul said: "God sent forth his Son, born of woman" (Gal 4:4). Origen commented: "Note well that he did not say, 'born *by means of* a woman' but 'born *of* a woman'" (*Comment on the Letter to the Galatians, PG* 14, 1298). This acute observation of the great exegete and ecclesiastical writer is important: in fact, if the Son of God had been born only "by means of" a woman, he would not truly have taken on our humanity, something which instead he did by taking flesh "of" Mary. Mary's motherhood, therefore, is true and fully human. The fundamental truth about Jesus as a divine Person who fully assumed our human nature is condensed in the phrase: "God sent forth his Son born of woman." He is the Son of God, he is generated by God and *at the same time* he is the son of a woman, Mary. He comes from her. He is *of* God and *of* Mary. For this reason one can and must call the Mother of Jesus the Mother of God [*Theotókos*].

Homily at First Vespers, Solemnity of Mary,
Mother of God
December 31, 2006

65. *Jesus, the Face of God*

God's Face took on a human face, letting itself be seen and recognized in the Son of the Virgin Mary, who for this reason we venerate with the loftiest title of "Mother of God." She, who had preserved in her heart the secret of the divine motherhood, was the first to see the face of God made man in the small fruit of her womb.

Homily on the Solemnity of Mary, Mother of God
January 1, 2010

66. *Mother of believers*

At Bethlehem, in the fullness of time, Jesus was born of Mary; the Son of God was made man for our salvation, and the Virgin became the true Mother of God. This immense gift that Mary has received is not reserved to her alone, but is for us all. In her fruitful virginity, in fact, God has given "to men the goods of eternal salvation . . . , because by means of her we have received the Author of Life" (cf. *Collect Prayer*). Mary, therefore, after having given flesh to the Only-Begotten Son of God, became the mother of believers and of all humanity.

Angelus
January 1, 2008

67. *Mother and teacher*

The mother is the one who gives life but also who helps and teaches how to live. Mary is a Mother, the Mother of Jesus, to whom she gave her blood and her body. And it is she who presents to us the eternal Word of the Father, who came to dwell among us.

Homily at First Vespers, Solemnity of Mary,
Mother of God
December 31, 2005

68. *Tent of the Word*

Mary, Mother of the Lord, truly teaches us what entering into communion with Christ is: Mary offered her own flesh, her own blood to Jesus and became a living tent of the Word, allowing herself to be penetrated by his presence in body and spirit. Let us pray to her, our holy Mother, so that she may help us to open our entire being, always more, to Christ's presence; so that she may help us to follow him faithfully, day after day, on the streets of our life.

Homily on the Solemnity of Corpus Domini
May 26, 2005

69. *Vocation*

[Mary] welcomed Jesus with faith and gave him to the world with love. This is also our vocation and our mission, the vocation and mission of the Church: to welcome Christ into our lives and give him to the world, so "that the world might be saved through him" (Jn 3:17).

Angelus
December 8, 2006

70. *Mother Church*

The Christian community, which in these days has remained in prayerful adoration before the crib, looks with particular love to the Virgin Mary, identifying itself with her while contemplating the newborn Baby, wrapped in swaddling clothes and laid in a manger. Like Mary, the Church also remains in silence in order to welcome and keep the interior resonances of the Word made flesh and in order not to lose the divine-human warmth that radiates from his presence. The Church, like the Virgin, does none other than show Jesus, the Savior, to everyone, and reflects to each one the light of his face, the splendor of goodness and truth.

Angelus
January 1, 2007

71. *History*

Such is the history of the Church: she began her journey in the lowly cave of Bethlehem, and down the centuries she has become a People and a source of light for humanity. Today too, in those who encounter that Child, God still kindles fires in the night of the world, calling men and women everywhere to acknowledge in Jesus the "sign" of his saving and liberating presence and to extend the "us" of those who believe in Christ to the whole of mankind.

Urbi et Orbi *message for Christmas*
December 25, 2009

VII. EPIPHANY

72. *The star*

The Magi set out because of a deep desire which prompted them to leave everything and begin a journey. It was as though they had always been waiting for that star. It was as if the journey had always been a part of their destiny, and was finally about to begin.

Meeting with Seminarians on the occasion of the
20th World Youth Day
August 19, 2005

73. *Seekers of truth*

On their journey, the star and the Sacred Scriptures were the two lights that guided the Magi, who appear to us as models of authentic seekers of the truth. They were Wise Men who scrutinized the stars and knew the history of the peoples. They were men of science in the broad sense, who observed the cosmos, considering it almost as a great open book full of divine signs and messages for human beings. Their knowledge, therefore, far from claiming to be self-sufficient, was open to further divine revelations and calls.

Angelus
January 6, 2010

74. *Inner journey*

The new King, to whom they now paid homage, was quite unlike what they were expecting. In this way they had to learn that God is not as we usually imagine him to be. This was where their inner journey began. . . . By serving and following him, they wanted, together with him, to serve the cause of good and the cause of justice in the world. In this they were right. Now, though, they have to learn that this cannot be achieved simply through issuing commands from a throne on high. Now they have to learn to give themselves—no lesser gift would be sufficient for this King. Now they have to learn that their lives must be conformed to this divine way of exercising power, to God's own way of being. They must become men of truth, of justice, of goodness, of forgiveness, of mercy. They will no longer ask: how can this serve me? Instead, they will have to ask: How can I serve God's presence in the world? They must learn to lose their life and in this way to find it.

Address during a youth vigil at the 20th World Youth Day
August 20, 2005

75. *I searched and I found*

Therefore, we can ask ourselves [following the example of the Magi]: what is the reason why some men see and find, while others do not? What opens the eyes and the heart? What is lacking in those who remain indifferent, in those who point out the road but do not move? We can answer: too much self-assurance, the claim to knowing reality, the presumption of having formulated a definitive judgment on everything closes them and makes their hearts insensitive to the newness of God. They are certain of the idea that they have formed of the world and no longer let themselves be involved in the intimacy of an adventure with a God who wants to meet them. They place their confidence in themselves rather than in him, and they do not think it possible that God could be so great as to make himself small so as to come really close to us. Lastly, what they lack is authentic humility, which is able to submit to what is greater, but also authentic courage, which leads to belief in what is truly great even if it is manifested in a helpless Baby. They lack the evangelical capacity to be children at heart, to feel wonder, and to emerge from themselves in order to follow the path indicated by the star, the path of God.

Homily on the Solemnity of the Epiphany of the Lord
January 6, 2010

76. Invitation

The example of the Magi of that time is also an invitation to the Magi of today to open their minds and hearts to Christ and to offer him the gifts of their research.

Homily on the Solemnity of the Epiphany of the Lord
January 6, 2007

77. Baptism of the Lord

The Feast of the Baptism of the Lord [concludes] the Liturgical Season of Christmas. . . . Baptism suggests very eloquently the global meaning of the Christmas celebrations in which the theme of *becoming God's children*, thanks to the Only-Begotten Son of God taking on our humanity, is a key element. He became man so that we might become children of God. God was *born* so that we might be *reborn*.

Angelus
January 10, 2010

VIII. PRAYERS

78. *Prayer for Christmas Eve*

Let us ask the Lord to grant us the grace of looking upon the crib this night with the simplicity of the shepherds, so as to receive the joy with which they returned home (cf. Lk 2:20). Let us ask him to give us the humility and the faith with which Saint Joseph looked upon the child that Mary had conceived by the Holy Spirit. Let us ask the Lord to let us look upon him with that same love with which Mary saw him. And let us pray that in this way the light that the shepherds saw will shine upon us too, and that what the angels sang that night will be accomplished throughout the world: "Glory to God in the highest, and on earth peace among men with whom he is pleased." Amen!

> *Homily on the Solemnity of the Nativity of the Lord*
> *December 24, 2006*

79. *Renew me*

Lord Jesus Christ, born in Bethlehem, come to us! Enter within me, within my soul. Transform me. Renew me. Change me, change us all from stone and wood into living people, in whom your love is made present and the world is transformed. Amen.

Homily on the Solemnity of the Nativity of the Lord
December 24, 2009

80. *Maraná, thá!*

Come, Lord Jesus! Come in your way, in the ways that you know. Come wherever there is injustice and violence. Come . . . wherever drugs prevail. Come among those wealthy people who have forgotten you, who live for themselves alone. Come wherever you are unknown. Come in your way and renew today's world. And come into our hearts, come and renew our lives, come into our hearts so that we ourselves may become the light of God, your presence. In this way let us pray with St. Paul: *Maranà, thà!* "Come, Lord Jesus!" and let us pray that Christ may truly be present in our world today and renew it.

General Audience
November 12, 2008

INDEX

(Numbering refers to the sequential positioning of each thought.)